S0-BOF-114

TO 2040

Also by JORIE GRAHAM

TO 2040

JORIE GRAHAM

COPPER CANYON PRESS

PORT TOWNSEND, WASHINGTON

Copyright 2023 by Jorie Graham
All rights reserved
Printed in the United States of America

Designed by Erica Mena.
Cover design by Gopa & Ted2, Inc.

Copper Canyon Press is in residence at Fort Worden State Park in Port Townsend, Washington, under the auspices of Centrum. Centrum is a gathering place for artists and creative thinkers from around the world, students of all ages and backgrounds, and audiences seeking extraordinary cultural enrichment.

LIBRARY OF CONGRESS CATALOGING-IN-PUBLICATION DATA
Names: Graham, Jorie, 1950- author.
Title: To 2040 / Jorie Graham.
Description: First edition. | Port Townsend, Washington : Copper Canyon
  Press, [2023] | Summary: "A collection of poems by Jorie Graham"—
  Provided by publisher.
Identifiers: LCCN 2022045410 (print) | LCCN 2022045411 (ebook) |
  ISBN 9781556596773 (hardback; acid-free paper) |
  ISBN 9781619322691 (epub)
Subjects: LCGFT: Poetry.
Classification: LCC PS3557.R214 T59 2023 (print) |
  LCC PS3557.R214 (ebook) | DDC 811/.54—dc23/eng/20221109
LC record available at https://lccn.loc.gov/2022045410
LC ebook record available at https://lccn.loc.gov/2022045411

98765432 FIRST PRINTING

COPPER CANYON PRESS
Post Office Box 271
Port Townsend, Washington 98368
www.coppercanyonpress.org

For Peter

CONTENTS

Like as the waves make towards the pebbl'd shore . . .

—Shakespeare

We are searching for the boats we forgot to build.

—Barry Lopez

Past midnight. Never knew such silence. The earth might be uninhabited.

—Samuel Beckett

TO 2040

I

ARE WE

extinct yet. Who owns
the map. May I
look. Where is my
claim. Is my history

verifiable. Have I
included the memory
of the animals. The animals'
memories. Are they

still here. Are we

alone. Look
the filaments
appear. Of memories. Whose? What was
land

like. Did it move
through us. Something says nonstop
are you here
are your ancestors

real do you have a
body do you have
yr self in
mind can you see yr

hands—have you broken it
the thread—try to feel the
pull of the other
end—says make sure

both ends are
alive when u pull to
try to re-enter
here. A raven

has arrived while I
am taking all this
down. In-
corporate me it

squawks. It hops
closer along the stone
wall. Do you remember
despair its coming

closer says. I look

at him. Do not
hurry I say but
he is tapping the stone
all over with his

beak. His coat is
sun. He looks
carefully at me bc
I am so still &

eager. He sees my

loneliness. Cicadas
begin. Is this a real
encounter I ask. Of the old
kind. When there were

ravens. No
says the light. You
are barely here. The
raven left a

long time ago. It
is traveling its thread its
skyroad forever now, it knows
the current through the

cicadas, which you cannot hear
but which
close over u now. But is it not
here I ask looking up

through my stanzas.
Did it not reach me
as it came in. Did
it not enter here

at stanza eight—& where

does it go now
when it goes away
again, when I tell you the raven is golden,
when I tell you it lifted &

went, & it went.

ON THE LAST DAY

I left the protection
of my plan & my
thinking. I let my self
go. Is this hope I

thought. Light fled.
We have a world
to lose I thought.
Summer fled. The

waters rose. How
do I organize
myself now. How do I
find sufficient

ignorance. How do I

not summarize
anything. Is this mystery,
this deceptively complex
lack of design. No sum

towards which to strive. No
general truth. None.
How do I go without
accuracy. How do I

go without industry.
No north or
south. What shall I
disrupt. How find

the narrowness. The
rare ineffable
narrowness. Far below
numbers. Through and behind

alphabets and their hiving, swarming—here,
these letters. I
lean forward
looking for the anecdote

which leads me closer to

the nothing. I do not

lack ideas. I do not
fail to see
how pieces
fall together. I do

not fail to be
a human companion
to the human. I am
not skeptical. I

am seeking to enter the in-
conspicuous. Where the stems
of the willows
bend when I

step. *There is dream in
them* I think. *There is
desire.* From this height
above the ground I see

too much. I need
to get down, need to
get out of the reach
of the horizon. Are

these tracks from this
summer or how many years
ago. Are these
grasses come again now,

new. This is being
remembered. Even as it
erases itself it does not
erase the thing

it was. And gave you.

No one can tell the whole story.

I

know myself I
say to my
self so I
cannot be

led astray. Led
astray I say I
know myself more
fully now so I

cannot be made
to do some-
thing I as
an other

wld never
do. But I
did it. Didn't I
do it. It wasn't

me to do such
a thing or believe
such a thing I
tell myself as I

look carefully into
the only mirror I
am given—my
self in there—me

looking carefully &
hard. I am honest in
my looking I
think as I see

someone else in there

opening, will in their
eyes wild like a sail
in the wind, wind
rising now as I

look in, be-
wildered. The old
gentleness where is
it. I put my hand

to my face but it
touches glass. Where
is my body to
guide me I

think. I tap at
the prisoner in
there, is that the
schoolroom, the

blank in the lesson,
is that my soul
gradually by its ten
thousand adjustments

to its own in-
creasing absence opening
too far. Is it blind. I
tap my face which is

gone on the glass which is
not gone. Don't stop
I hear my mind hiss,
don't stop for

anything.

I AM STILL

on the earth.
My interval
is fixed. Who
fixed it.

For a while
all that came out
was answers.
Then nothing.

In the distance
high tension lines
on fire and up close
a knot in a

branch on
fire. Stumps
everywhere. I waited. Looked for
a crease in the earth

wind or light
could course in
guiding us, pointing
the way. Any

way. Sought
spells. Climbed higher
onto the ridge to see
further. Rocks

burning in the
distance. Then distance
burning. No
sweetwater. All tongues

fire, no speech
those of us human
could read for
signs. Grant me

mission my rushed heart
said. Grant me vision
into the balance
sheet. Everywhere I looked

those still traversing
began to fail. Air they
limped in itself
limped—

I thought I detected a
rhythm in the reddening—
thought *at least pattern
give me*—but

dust jerked-up in a
circle then dropped
holding no ghost
of meaning. Thought

are those still
bldngs in the distance—
are those still
addresses. *The air* I sd out

loud, looking into it standing there
in front of me. The air
going into its far moments
without

gathering-up. Smooth.
Flowing. Unruffled.
Above, new crowds now
crossing the summit &

swarming out into
the valley desperate for
intention. Which way
do we go

I ask the air. What
is it coughs in the
invisible, in the as-yet
unmade, as-yet un-

forced. Where nothing has been
established.
No forms locked
in. The sun

comes up burning.
Say everything I say to the air
which begins to
thin now, say

everything before it dis-
appears. Turn us
loose. I remember
a stream darting free

from headwaters & then the

downslope which was
earth's gift. I remember it
widening. Leaves stirring above it,
as-if leaves stirring deep in-

side its
surface. What
are they an
expression of

I think as I squint them

in—gripping before
this memory
fades. Oh. Try to hold on.
We are a reflection

now. Where is what we

reflect? How could it
leave us here. Old
story, have you ended.
Have you left us in this memory-

stream now, without
reasons, without
plot. I look up before the
air becomes unbreathable,

I close my eyes and try to see it again,
the stream. It is a temple. It is
rushing. How could we
not have heard.

TRANSLATION RAIN

I am writing this in code because I cannot speak or say
the thing. The thing which should be, or I so wish
could be
plumbed fathomed disinterred from this silence, this ever thickening
silence through which, once, the long thin stalks & stems, first
weaker weeds then branching &
stiffening, steadying &
suddenly sturdier—
strong enough to carry the seen—*the seeming* autocorrect reminds me—
the meaning my mind offers rushing in here
such that I must pull it back here—
grew. They, or is it *it*
grew. I
turn to the dead more now,
clearer every day as I approach them,
there in their silky layers of
silence, their wide almost waveless ocean,
rolling under their full moon,
swells striating the horizonless backdrop,
extending what seems like forever
in that direction—
though what can forever mean where there is
no space no time. I breathe
that in
and stare at it. I breathe,
I have an *in* and
out. I should have mentioned earlier this autocorrected to
breed. I had thought to ignore it but what a strange thing
how we expanded,
spread ourselves in smaller and smaller bits
across the natural world
until we were so thin with participation we

fell away.

Remember the code says the away.

But I was saying

how finally the rain will come. *Finally it will* I say in the code—&

you do intuit my meaning do you

not. It is a rain I have waited for all my life—

why do I see it only

now for what it

is—yes bronze as the sun tries to hang on—

then all these platinums braiding its freedoms,

coursing to find every crevice, loosen every

last stitch &

go in. It will touch everything. It will make more of the

more. More says my baffled soul, yes more.

It will push itself through & more deeply through till *all* must grow.

And yet we pray for it.

We thought it would never come.

Something *did* come says the code.

But *it* did not come.

Not in reality.

We thought it was an ideal.

Therefore it must come.

But it did not come.

How I wish I could say *free*. And yet we are not free it

seems. Or are we.

Each word I use I have used before.

Yet it is not used, is it? It is not used up, is it? Because what is in it stays

hidden. And the words

appear again as if

new. *Rain*, I say. *Rain now.*

And the black ocean shows itself in infinite detail because of the moon.

No matter that all is not lit.

Much remains because much remains hidden.

And you, are you there in the hidden—

nothing is rare,

all gleams.
And you there, gather these words up now & store them as seed.
Wait for the next rain.
In the world we lost there are those who knew if the lifesaving
rain would
come in time—if it would
actually fall—not pass us by again as a prediction, as
mist. They knew from
the birds. I
am still here with the birds for this while longer.
I do not know what they say.
Dust rises.
Evening sets.
I listen to the chatter.
I remember the clatter of sudden rain. The clapping of it onto the
hard soil.
The birds roost.
Among them a silence now & one singer briefly singing. Then silence.
We must all wait together.
There is no way to know.
It did not come.

TO 2040

With whom am I speaking, are you one or many, *what* are u, are u, do I make my-
self clear, is this which we called speech what u use, are u a living form such as the
form I inhabit now letting it speak me. My window tonight casts light onto the snow,
I cast from my eye a glance, a touchless touch, tossed out to capture this shine we

cast. I pull it in, into my memory store. I have lost track. It's snowed for more
than we'd imagined at the start, it began, unexpectedly it began, it did not really
cease again, it slowed some days, melted as it fell on some, days passed thru snow
rather than snow thru days. Did it remember us at some point, when we cld hold no

more memory of day in mind. We had started with minutes. We had loved their
fullness—cells flowing thru this body of time—purging all but their passing thru us
& our letting them flow-through. But then they stopped being different. You
couldn't tell one minute from another, or an hour, day, year. Years pulled their

lengths through us like long wet strings, and we hung onto them, they strung us a
ways along, & up, they kept us from drowning in the terrible minutes. Once I sat
down & cried as I watched the sun come up & the flakes falling as if not noticing the
movmt from night into day—at least let there be difference—otherwise whatever

remains of desire will go—otherwise there will be nothing I have saved—nothing to
save—make day flower as a piece of time again—it's cold—dream is a hard thing to
catch sight of—I said *dream*—*I said dream* what is it I said—I said it because just
now, looking out, it's a reflex, I saw, as if a stain or residue of scent, a yellowing on

snow in patches, long thin stretches, like a very cold face remembering something it
wishes to forget, I saw a poverty touched by a lessening of poverty, a memory of a
chime on cold air, a strange flash as of birdshadow—so fast—though there are no
birds any longer—longer—I would have said *ever again*—but then there it is that

word I dread so—again—here where we have none of it or nothing but, we can't
tell—but it was the so-rare poking-through of the strange sun we have—& for
an instant it gave us shadows—branches that do not move moved—against snow,
wall, pane, against trunk, intertwining & trembling inside other shadows, & all

was alive. You feel the *suddenly*. You feel like an itch a thing you used to call so
casually yr *inwardness*, u feel yr looking at the knotting, the undoings of nothing in
nothing, gorgeous—cursive golds what wld u say now, say it now, do it now yr in-
wardness thinks as you feel yr greed in yr eyes yr hands yr soul—how u drink

what used to be just end-of-day, low light, any winter afternoon. Give me a day back.
Give the slowing of dusk into gloaming. Give me a night. Shut something down, close
your fist over it, hold us tight, then unclench unfurl slowly release us again into light.
Give us a dawn. Give us the one note without warning where one call one cry breaks

& darkness releases a branch & if you wait the whole crown then the body will be
unhidden and handed over into yr sight. The sight of the watching human. I turn
back-in as the accident the release of light is fixed & we are back in snowlight now.
How far forward r we. We used to speak of future. Speech had a different function

then. It's hard to know when to break the silence now. It has something to do with
the absence of night. We never knew we shld feel the rotation. We hurled
forward. Yes towards death but what joy. Didn't know it was a game. Should have
loved the hurtling, the losses, the hurry dilation delay fear surprise fury. We miss

the sense of abandonment yes we miss homesickness. We miss the vector in any
direction. You back there are you back there listening to me am I audible what do I
do to make this audible don't forget to ask when your time comes for *presence*.
Do not ask for forgiveness. Do not ask for youth. They will offer them up

pristine and innocent. Do not listen. Do not make the silly mistake do
not ask for eternity. Look behind you, turn, look down as much as you can, notice all
that disappears. Place as much as you can in your heart. It doesn't matter what's in
your mind. When you come here all you will be left w/is a heart they spill out, a

tin cup, they count up what you put in it, they shake it into a small burlap sack, they weigh it, they tie it up, they do not give it back. It is then you are placed at your window to watch. Then the snow begins. You are told to remember the message u accidentally forgot to attend to. It is among the things they sequestered when they

measured u. You must sit now and recall the message. The one put in yr hand but not opened. You were busy. There was little time. Little notice was given. Its ink is new. The fold in its paper single & crisp. The words glow in their crease. The unread shines with its particular shine. It has been weighed. It was put to yr account &

burned. What was it, u must remember, what was yr message, what were u meant to pass on?

THEY ASK ME

why the new
flawless birds
wired to perfection
whose beauty

song flight lift
hover settle you
cannot tell from
those not coming

back are not the
same, whose
feathertips shine
as if in the old

sunlight, whose
speckled wings
mottle further with
perfect shadow-speckle,

whose necks have
the sweet up/down
jerk of worry, whose
throat is made to

throb so slightly
as was the case
when song was
expelled why

do they not satisfy
us, why it is
only if we shut our
eyes the trills—

you can choose
the kind of bird—are
real, they come
to our sills, they leave

unexpectedly bc we
move…How they
flocked up across our
fields. How

that last morning,

in that world, in rising ground-

mist, in the pull of its fast
evaporation as that strange
sun rose, arms
outstretched &

laughing, out of
breath, we ran to chase them
till they dis-
appeared.

DUSK IN DROUGHT

Tongues in dusk
air are bats but I try
to remember
larks. Bushes are taken

away and replaced by

sounds & circuits of
mind where those sounds get
lost—pavilions,
mazes—so clean—crumbs all

gone now—also visits to
anyone or
anything
gone—though we

still feel we
can hear them
staccato frequencies
before they finally enter us

for good. Then it is night.

What do we know now.
The wind comes up.
Grief is a form
which can shape this

if you want a shape.
But you can also sit here
a long time
without ever again

needing a shape. It
is not easy. I
cannot say I know
how it's done. But

it's done. Wait & it
will be completely
done. And then
there's no more cost

& you fall

neither down nor
thru. Then—that's
it. *Breathe the dry air
in* my heart tells me—

don't make the mistake.
Breathe. Yes
the drought is everywhere out there
but in the night

the stems of stars mist-up
just enough for u to recall
when there was
humanity, humidity, & the stars

dangle, sting. Ah there is
no return
is there. I wish I could
address you. I loved

so many
things—sitting by the window on
the train, thinking of death as if it were
a sweetness, a kind of

love, saying *snow*

as snow fell fast against our hurtling
forwardness—all of it postcard
colored—shaggy trees flying by—
us hoping for *pitch black night* and imagining the *beauty*

of a journey with
no return. I wish I knew
whom to address
this time. Don't be the fool

loving the sparks of
yr engines, yr micro-
transformers, don't think you can put off
that evening walk now because there's trouble to fix,

there's someone to love,
there's a need to postpone
escape. Let me tell you,
there *is* a guard. Yes he's a servant too

but he's yr guard.
Don't let down yr guard.
Perform yr aliveness every
instant for him, & cheerfully,

keeping him fascinated
so he doesn't accidentally
fall asleep on yr
watch, or they will bring in the papers with

the diagnosis, the temperature
read-outs, the projected
wind speeds. And the sand
will begin to arrive

as if out of thin air. Yes.
Now,
what is it still lies undisturbed
on the surface of

your mind? What is that
attached to your hands? A moth
stops in the air
before u, look

closely into its book, a rule is
applied, look closely into that manual,
into the book of
tools no longer

used, into the book of
what we don't yet see
under this applause of
starlight for the always

finishing play unfurling
right before our very
eyes. Are they
open or

shut. A brief shower coalesces but

as always
passes. A fly is rubbing its
head with its wings
in the dark. The disappearing watertable

is not entirely
silent if I am completely
still. Listen: I am
completely still.

II

DIS-

ease came. Dis-
figurement. Dis-
enfranchisement, dis-
sembling, dis-

grace. Now
who am I
going to be I
asked. Whom does one

ask, you might
ask. Are you
still alive there,
reading these words,

is the beautiful air

still shoving its
fistfuls
into my
lungs. In-

hale says the nurse,
holding my hand.
Try again says
another voice

further away. Try
harder. Do you
remember what it is
to try. Do you

remember when u took yr
first breath. You are there
again now
says the voice

on the speaker.
Did they raise the
volume or raise
their voice. It's

cold. I can't
remember why it is we
love. I can't remember
why it is we

breathe. One more time,
says the monitor,
let's try living here
one more time—

how will this time
be different I
ask, what are
my reasons, what are

my duties, where
is the rewritten
rulebook…Then my crow,
my singularity

began to appear. He is

a manifestation
I want to say but
my throat is
narrowing, vocal cords

slipping. The walls
are wings now. The ob-
servation window
his beak. The lit up

monitors gazing at me
without kindness
or unkindness—& when he flaps his wings
I will dis-

appear I think—no,
when I hear their sharp wind
all this will
go. I will be wild again,

I will be taken in.
Please try again
he says from the
booth. We need

you to wager
everything
on us again. We need u to
invent god like a razor

& have him slice open
all this nothingness around us,
we need to watch it
lay before us,

slain. We need wins &
losses. The walls which are wings
shake a little now,
as if all of us

in this drama are
inconsolable. The booth
chokes though I realize it's
backfeed

from the only
mic. Pls
try to breathe again
the voice clearing its throat says—

can it really have been
crying—or u will
never be here again
it whispers, though it seems

an order. Fascination
fills the empty room. All the sterile
implements & cables
gleam. I do not want

to bear witness
anymore I say. It is
impossible. There is no
story. But the eye

of my raven in the
booth, behind the partition,
takes a bite out of
my voice. It does not

blink, it does not acknowledge
the passage of
time, it just peers &
overgrows me with layers of

glances,
till I'm bodied again,
till I'm thick, & it's saying
you are in history dear child

you are only in history,

you are not in time,
& you're not getting
out. Not yet. Not
in time. You

have to return here
right now & watch it all dis-
integrate. Find
the door

out, the hum pleads.
Out of the future I ask
trying to rise. *No,*
out to the future it murmurs

as hope smiles
its wry smile—
stay in touch it is
saying, stay in touch

babe. I'm here
for u. I'm always
going to be
here for you.

I CATCH SIGHT OF THE NOW

unforgettable though then hardly noticed green
tiled ledge
just up to my right in the glistening shower-stall, slightly above my open
eyes, square window in it, & slender citrine
lip onto which I place, gently, this first handful of hair—always I see it—the window-
pane up there letting anything in and out that
wishes to pass
thru—so freely—drops from the steam of the shower
on it, the slipping of forever & for-
ever all down the
pane, where, beyond the still-wet clump, *all* seems to shine and
murmur it's just day, just this day, another day, filled with the only
of this minute, this split minute, in which if I
reach now I can feel
the years, the fissure in them,
these fractions here inside the
instant—oh mine—how mine—now moving so
differently, as if entering a room with frozen fingers and they say
no, no you cannot warm them here
at the fire
there is no fire, there is no
room, actually there is nothing, though you can
start carving the nothing, you can test your strength
against the nothing, the subject is
loss, the dark is inside your
open mouth not knowing what else there is again to
say, a kind of howling without
sorrow, no amazement, no
wisdom, just the roomlessness of this your *suddenly*—
suddenly everything, suddenly there is no more of what there
was, suddenly you do not die of fear you just fear, suddenly
there is no such thing as right or wrong yr hand is

a claw full of hair there is no
purification anywhere as the shower keeps streaming looking for
hollows, more hollows, this thread of the only
water cycle dragged down
into here to
run all over you, to rake yr
skinny neck & down inside of you where you
look up, open yr
mouth—to scream to sing to say the one
right word—as now the next
soft handful
comes, it is such a surprise, as you raise up yr
hand, high, full, to the ledge, to pile it on there—& what
will you do
now, shooting your gaze into those filaments, your years of having & not
knowing, still wet, in clumps, through which the daylight now is
pouring itself,
though it is not pouring anything at all or into
anything at all because it's just the planet
turning again and again into and out of the
dark which is not itself actually dark
at all.

DAY

Here it comes now, at the last, the woodpecker.
It's come from afar.
It's put its beak in above my heart.
Lie still it says.
Very still.
Listen.
You loved the light, it says, of day.
You let it touch yr face all yr life & u never apologized, never felt
the distance in it—its howling—its gigantic
memory. You did not bury yr face in yr hands,
in the soil, in the grass with
gratitude. Something warbled.
Something flew past
in the air—a ravine quietly opened—water
deep in the earth narrowly
darted between rocks to
reach you. It was
wild. Your blood
took violent turns
left and right inside you—it gave you
time—
Now it drops
its needle in deeper.
You are dying it says. Maybe today,
maybe another. Rain is starting somewhere,
it's coming down fast it says,
I'm busy it says,
I'm attending to shorelines I'd like to save,
its body like a small golden trombone,
its crest like a fretboard day cld be thrumming—as they are
friends—we're from the same
district, it explains, we share hometowns,

we don't want to ruin your day but we're
busy. The needle is turning in me again.
It wants to play music I imagine.
It too wants to live its brief glorious moment,
right to the end please,
as a civilization might also like if possible,
right to the end,
the very end.
Is there a *right* end I ask the bird
as it bows from the waist over me, as if starting
to dance while
digging in deeper,
widening and opening the hole
in my heart,
dust all over the floor from its work.
What would have given you enough, it asks,
working furiously,
I think its face is puffed from the effort,
is daylight coming back again
for me I
ask, as someone adjusts the pillow under my head,
is this the end of the second
movement or the third
it says to the air—
do you still have another round of day in you?—
as they pull a wet cloth
over my eyes—
to clean them out I hope to myself,
that I might see once more
a bit of the something that blues-in softly
after furious night,
is that a nurse now pulling at my neck,
is that a window coming clear or is it blank wall,
are those letters in the air spelling something firm even
possibly urgent
or are they just the bits & pieces of shadow

the pre-dawn world tosses
flagrantly around,
wasting nothing but making it feel
as if there were plenty, overmuch, endless—oh way more than enough to be
wildly wasted. I lift up my palm
and stare at it
as per usual,
as I have done for a thousand years,
& this nightgown believe me it is not satin
although it too makes its little music.
February 2022 I'm singing you out,
if nothing else let me finish my song.
I'm not enough but I
could have been less.
When he is done he cranes up and stares.
His crest is stupendous.
His stare is righteous.
You must have come from somewhere far away I think
as I've never seen the likes of you
around me
anywhere.
What do you think your strength is for it asks—
what do u think yr intelligence is.
Surgical clips blink.
They imitate day.
Was it my strength which was my mistake, I ask,
yr back is golden and red,
yr feathers stretch into every direction, they point,
u could be mosaic, yr gold seems chipped from
what used to be Venice,
Torcello specifically, in the old world,
yr legs are rolled tight
into their sacred scrolls—
oh you're done with something—I'm not sure what,
you're done with the warnings & the

proclamations,
yr notebook is overflowing with second
chances. Now it is
silent. It has moved up. It pecks at the bone
at the back of my neck.
I lift my arm up
to try to
touch.
No pity anywhere.
It's then I hear it, the first bird breaking
what used to be dawn.
Will you let me hear it?
What will you hear this time it asks.
What will you make of the chorus
when it comes.
What will you make.
You had a lifetime
to get this story,
to write its long and bitter poem.
You had thousands of hearts, one for each day
which let you into its cool new body,
for free,
unstopped.
What will you make.
I saw you turn away.
I watched you arrange and rearrange your minutes.
Lie back down now.
Be very still.
I do not know
if you will be entertained again.
And he left then.
There was no weeping, just feathers passing.
And I am here now listening for day
with all I've got.
What have I got.

IN REALITY

the river was still widening as it went, as it carried me, thick mists rising
off it all day,
was still widening, yes, for a while longer, holding
the sky in its belly and back,
me on my back in the small of
my boat, rudder jammed, oar
lost or is it I tossed it
some long time ago
when I imagined myself
to be free. In the distance I see, reflected in the spooling,
a pair of spyglasses lifted
by the surveyor—fitted out for life—and it seems he is laughing
at what he sees, so magnified, light splaying over the surfaces,
the smeared faces of kings
whose lands are now vanquished,
clouds folding in the waters their rolled-up blankets
no longer needed for the ceremonies, the dancing,
controlling ebb, controlling
flow,
& like candy the benzenes the tankers before me have trailed,
& like wedding veils the foam made of monies,
a few millennia of monies,
no slack in that accrual,
no slowdown in that accumulation—we were fitted out
for life, armed with evolution & imitation,
trees casting their calligraphies deeper and deeper as they try to tell
the story of the bend we are now
approaching. A parrot flew over. It crossed the whole
river. I took a moment to sit up and
watch. Took in the setting. Took in the
dead forest, the ruined brick smokestack just visible
from a clearing, some columns still standing beyond it

someone's unyielding idea of
happiness.
Everything hangs in the balance, say the looping vines
the late red light begins articulating. Think about it, they scrawl,
try to remember
what it was you loved, try to clean up your memories
in time. The dragonflies begin as I lie back down.
I try to recall how I've gotten this far.
Every wing in the swarm also benzene-rainbowed
& clouding me
as we round the bend—& everywhere their eyes, their thousands of eyes.
They see nothing we see I think, and
am I a ghost now,
my left eye stung shut,
my right eye trying to make out what's up ahead
as the light goes gold.
Isn't it beautiful the old world says.
I try to remember. My one eye weeps.
Along the bank I make out the easels now. I see smocks and palettes,
and always that one hand up in the air
tapping & pointing, caressing the emptiness
through which whatever it is
they are seeking
arrives. Then down it goes
onto its canvas.
Represent me says the day. Quick. There's no time to lose.
Represent my million odors.
Represent my shaking grasses
where the wind picks up and the river narrows and the dream of forgiveness is replaced
by desire.
Forgive me I think as the silt everywhere widens.
The light is failing. The dried banks show through.
Now the surveyor is packing his tools.
I feel his gaze cross my forehead inadvertently, feel the painter's gaze
brush my eyes without knowing.
The smoke from the dead stack is filling the river,

though it's just the riverbed coming up to meet us.
The lover of dead things flies by gingerly.
First bats swing across so absent of greed.
I look down at my hands, the air shrieking a little.
I figure the new swarms will be mosquitoes.
I lie in my going. I have nothing to contribute.
The world was always
ready for the world.
The river is running thin.
I see the fish on the banks with no birds around them.
Human heart, I say to myself, what are you doing here, this is far too much
for you to lay
eyes on.
The young fish float in the brackish water.
The slowing current. The cries of the dusk birds like shattering glass,
one cry and they're done.
To whom am I singing.
The winning ticket is still in my pocket.
The disappearing lovers are still in my satchel.
I have the stories we needed ready.
I understand the comings and goings called grief.
It is then that I see the river is ending.
The dusk hits its silver.
It thinks it's a jackpot.
The water is down to a handful of jewels
tossed out here and there on the miles of dry sand.
That's all I recall.
Then the keel hits and I'm tipped over gently,
as if to be fully & finally
poured out.
I am told by the cracks in the sand the whole length of the bed
to get up now, to *gather*
belongings. I am told to hurry & join the line,
to take my place, prepare my
ticket, & if I have a chance
to *choose*

disappearance. Told I might still get lucky,
might still get out.
Out to where, I wonder, looking back at my skiff,
at the millions of hulls
in this dried bend,
supplies strewn everywhere on the dead bed,
flashlights in dusklight picking us out.
Almost invisible, the plastics gleam…
Thus it was we came to no longer reach the ocean.
Flow rate failed. Flow direction failed. Surface water dis-
appeared. Subsurface
dried. I remember the spring, the headwaters, precipitation, swell.
I see again the currents
begin—the sweet cut into land of
channels, meanders. Remember the
turns. Put my hands
in the springs,
the groundwater recharge. The slow delicate fanning
of the drainage basin. The mouth, the confluence,
the downriver arrivals—
delta—sediment yield—salt tide—
open sea.

CAN YOU

hear yourself
breathe. Can you help
me. Can you
hear the fly. Can you

hear the tree. No
I don't mean wind,
I mean the breathing of
the tree through

bark. Can u, say the grasses,
please hear
us. Can we hear u hear
the tips of water on

us, lithe &
so heavy with light & bending
lens-tips. Can u
hear this e-

vaporation. Can u
keep
blessing, keep not
thinking, remind

yourself of

your own

breathing, & what
is growing—leaves root sap, sun
forcing the flower....
Moving this way

you'll see you can hear
soil breathe,
& in it, working to get thru it,
the worm,

& each turning of it
by the worm, hear, &
the breathing in it
of the worm, hear. Moving this way

you'll hear the earth go on
without you—
when u are
no longer

here, when u are

not breathing. The fish the
water the sand the
needle in the pine. The here. Hear it
breathing

as it turns,
and as now in it turns
the effort
of this worm.

THE VR

mask is strapped on now. The rubber brace
goes round my
face then neck, they slip it on fast, it's cold, then it
snaps on. They've put
the clamp in my mouth
so I can't bite off
my own tongue
in amazement. Amazement
comes. Hello it says. Here I am. There is an arm, look, a tiny arm
on the dirt road, yes, it's dirt after all, the
road, I pick it
up, it fits in my palm,
it's coated with dust but I make out the lines of
destiny, they are cracked,
the line of fate is
curved,
trying to turn around on the field of the palm,
like a river when there were rivers
and geologic time,
the arm like something that grew up fast, out of dry soil, as if it *were* soil, or once
soil and breath,
when there was myth, when there was
the fantasy of
creation,
but it's my arm &, see now, it fits back on my shoulder as
my very arm, something I
own—you saw it
with your very own
eyes they say, *did you not*, the row of poplars dividing my field from
someone else's
stirs, & I see how the trees want to run, how they want to be barefoot, how their roots
feel bloody to them though they seem

so clean, so innocent & willing, so planted, to
us, from
here, I detect in them a terrible need for power, for action which might require
judgment, forgiveness,
we are not alone says the minister of the mask,
everyone wants to know
suffering, otherwise what is there
to remember & forget,
how cold the straps feel, they read my mind, things turn warm out of
nowhere, there must be no
monotony says the voice, would you like the dust turned to mud, shall we give
the trees wings, go ahead, use your arm now,
here is another for the other side,
you might not have noticed it too was ripped off
in your prior order,
and indeed there it is, so still in the mud now,
the ring still gleaming on its finger gives it away, I could have stepped on it I
say, I hear cicadas even though it is cold, how
real, how real?, we are returning to some prior place
where we will find everything as it should have been,
the evenings shall be the evenings,
the sun shall be warm but not too warm—there will be gazes in the eyes of creatures
which will be recognizable to us, not fear, not all the time hunger & fear,
there will be time for curiosity,
there will be children, and time, the creatures will not avert their eyes, the rain
will come again and we will hear it fall
on our roofs—now *they* are making rain fall, they are making a soft wind
cross the field,
they have placed flowers in the crevices, and fruits in the trees,
for the time being,
for just when we are peering
in that direction,
look, the place where the chemical factory was before the world disappeared
is full of wheat, and doors seem to open
as I approach.
The strap tugs. We are still perfecting the desires

they say. Look there's a feather on the dust I say. A bird
passed over. I can put it on now. Like
this. Look I am wearing it, the feather. I shall plunge it in my
back, I can make it be
huge. Now it is I
who pass
over. But I am still
here. The path is filled with torn-out
feathers. It is soft. Dust rises. Are they gone. Are the minders
no longer in this
story. Am I alone here. Am I just
here
now. Look it is the scene of
destruction I think. Something was
caught here & it
fought hard here &
lost. Where is the antagonist. Oh is it
me I think, putting my hand down now
in the down, in the piles of down, where it
fought off something like me &
lost its fight.

III

CAGE

They ask me why. They ask me again
why. Why the *last* of. Why the last of
a time. See, it curls up in the doorway & is
the doorway. Then wind and snow and time—your only time—
curl up in it. Then the howling. It's saying
see, here, in this doorway, look respectfully, it is yr cage. Saying here is
yr opening
that cannot be
filled, these holes where yr ears
should be, where yr eyes shld be, everything
blows through—yr set of wrong answers, yr insufficient offerings,
something not even fire could
burn—all exhalation, sprawl, flow—emptiness
making of itself a shape for a *while,*

why a while—because a while—that

is the subject—cannot be depicted—u

hold your hands up thinking u are

opened, u are not—u are still shut—completely shut—all

must go through u—shriek, mutter yr
name, no one
can hear u—it's yr cage, it's leaking everywhere, lacking
everything—the shape of poverty is time, the form of time is
poverty, we
starve, you've no idea how fast we
starve. Are we lost? Isn't it just waiting. Just *like*
waiting. *Full of* waiting? Look, a little sunlight strikes this sill, these
bars, they gleam. It's even a bit
beautiful—isn't

it—this dream of being held while the light flows
through us. Look at that latch.
This is America look close. No one wants u
to struggle. Sit still. Wait. Feel about,
they must have left food. They usually do. *My*
home, you can say. Grip the bars and feel their tenderness. They mean
well. They mean
to keep you safe.That's why they
shine the way they do. Maybe they're
angels the wind screams coming and going. Maybe there's a string & if u
pull it hard a bulb will light
somewhere up there, there might be
stairs, an exit up, but no,
don't think, you cannot turn, don't
crane. That rotting smell is of the too-much-thought.
Did that. Sacrificed that. Centuries. We're done. Are we not
done. Lick your fingers. Keep
your feet warm. This is home now. No more
voyaging. That's over now.
You have made the exchange.
You have made the agreement re wildness,
remember? You traded it in, your tongue,
remember? In here it's all about the littlest
trick you've learned, remember? You
are just supposed to say *yes*. Just that. You say it well
without a tongue. And you must train
yr listening now. Not much
to hear but there cld still be
just enough: as in hear this: the moment after. Your moment
after. Touch it. Go ahead. *After what*?
It does not matter after what. It's just the after. Yes
it hurts. What do you mean by
forgotten. I mean
not enough. Who is this
speaking. I am the not enough. I am
all you have said. I am yr passageway. You are being shoved
thru—*as if swaying* they would like u to say, *as if*

dancing—oh dancing—but no, you are shoved
thru—the mind can't help—wonder fingers the
lock—latch says *feel me*, says
u are being recorded,
put your hands where I can see them,
where are your hands where are your eyes,

give yourself up, comply, quickly comply, the wind can't do a

thing, the light can't see, the blossoming exit-wound keeps hissing *sing*.

TIME FRAME

The American experiment will end in 2030 she said
looking into the cards,
the charts, the stars, the mathematics of it, looking
into our palms, into all of our
palms, into the leaves at the
bottom of
the empty cup—searching its emptiness, its piles of dead
bodies or is it grass at the edge
of the field where the abandoned radio is crackling
at the winter-stilled waters, the winter-killed
will of God—in the new world now the old world—
staring quietly without emotion into the rotten meat
in the abandoned shops, moving aside with one easy gesture
the broken furniture, the fourth wall
smashed
& all
the private lives of the highrise apartments
exposed to the city then
wind. Ash everywhere. The sounds of
crying. Loud then
soft. It will not seem like it's
dying
right away, she said. What is the "it" you refer to I
ask. Is it a place. Is it
an idea. A place is
an idea, an idea is for a while a place. Look
she says, there are
two fates. One is the idea one is the place.
And everywhere I see water.
As in blessing? As in baptism?
As in renewal? No,
as in the meadows disappear under the sea.
Then I heard a sound in the far

distance where her gaze rested. Are those
drums? Are we in the distant past or the distant
future I ask. The witches float in the air
above us. There are three. Of
course there are three. They have returned. No,
your ability to see them
has returned. Your
willingness. She asked for
cold wine and a railway schedule. It was time
she said, to move on, her gaze
looking out at the avenues and smaller streets,
at the silk dresses on the mannequins in
storefronts, all of them, across the
planet, the verandas poking out under the
hemlocks, violin strings crossing from
one century to another, although now I could hear they were
sirens all along,
invisible and desperate the warnings
in their rise & fall—
are you not listening
are you not listening—
yes those are sirens in the streets but here,
up close, in the recording of the
orchestra, the violin solo
has begun, it is screaming from one
ruined soul to another to beware, to pull the
bloody bodies from the invisible
where we are putting them daily—
no, every minute, no,
faster—we are o-
bliterating the one chance we had to be
good. There it is. The word. It brings us up
short. I notice she is gone. The
American project she had said, putting the words
out into the kitchen air with some measure of
kindness. It was not the only one, she sd, but it was

the last one.
After it, time ran out. We both looked out the window
still shocked by the beauty of the moonlight
in this Spring. Are we running out
of Springs I had wanted to
ask. Is the oxygen. Will there be no more open
channels. Can one not live
beneath. A little life in the
morning. Crazed police cars in the distance
but here this sunflower
which seeded itself,
seeded its mathematics & religion in our tiny
backyard,
will do. The creaking
doorhandle we love,
the spider we help come back after each wind
by letting the hanging vine
which needs to be trimmed
just stay—*just stay* I whisper to myself—
stay under, don't startle
time, the century
will go by—you can mind
your own business. You can finger the rolled up
leaf, feel its veins, you can watch the engines go by
over all the bridges
above you.
You can remain unassimilated. The
American project she said, will end
in 2030. Said find land away from here. Find
trustworthy water.
Have it in place
by then. I paid her.
I saw the bills go into the pocket
in her purse. Her shoes were so worn.
Her terror was nowhere. I looked at my garden.
It was dry here and there.
The shoots were starting up. Like a

dream they were poking through the rusty
fence.
I am spending my life, I thought. I am un-
prepared. It is running thru
my fingers. The wind is
still wild. My bones hurt sometimes
causing pain. It is not terror.
I feel for the cash in my pocket.
I do not have time to prepare.
I am comfortable.
Time passes and I am still here. I am
getting by. I replace one
calendar with another. I put seed out
for birds and sometimes one
comes. Once I saw two.
The spider is still here. I remember how geese
used to fly over. It meant something.
I remember when there were planes
& I could see them catch the light up there. What a
paradise. Some people had
enough. They were not happy but they were
able to come and go
at will.
They could leave
their houses. At any time. Anytime. And go
where they wished. Sometimes
we shared ideas. It
filled the time. We agreed or we did not.
They were not afraid. I was not
afraid. Summer would come soon.
It would get warmer. It might rain too hard.
When it flooded we worked to fix it.
We did as we saw fit.
Hi neighbor we would say across the fence
to the one tending their portion of the
disaster.
It will be ok again soon,

one of us would say. We were allowed to
speak then. It was permitted.
One of us might dream. One of us might
despair. But we cleaned up the
debris together & the next day sun came
& we were able to sit in it
as long as our hearts desired.

FOG

Then the drone came. A small personal drone. Hung at an
intimate height. Had
much to say. Hovering,
eye to eye, lurching &
chattering. Is it your time now, I thought. Thought
it said
you should have learned to
love but came up
close, saw it was old, had been
patched thousands of
times, maybe more, was medalled with debris,
a tin castle, a wooden fish, a rattle—a plastic
clock w/one hand—piano strings w/hooks—a miniature
telephone pole—a brass
templefront & golden ladder stuck
in a tiny
well—all shaking the air—a tinny racket—
also scraps of veil—maybe tulle—seemed angry—one eye a milagro
hanging there sideways—a pair of
lungs or were those actual
air sacs & bronchial
tubes—
the red drops actual—
as if whistling or singing though we both were
silent. I have seen everything it said, though I could actually hear
nothing. *Of the*
old order, it said.
Hear the silence.
Underfoot the tree roots surfaced & ran across earth. I felt them
in my instep. All was
dry. Said I have seen good and evil, they cancel each other out till there is

nothing, love it. Said
there is not much left now you can
use, use being yr
thing. Leaves
blew across the path The whole
path rattled. Could it be tanks I thought. But it was just wind. *Just
wind?* the wind said.
Air parted round the drone as it spoke.
We have killed &
killed, I am tired, I come from an old
way which will be disappeared
soon, ask why you are here,
people fought over me, it wasn't me, I was always just
sadness—but they did not know
how much they would
regret
everything they did—
everything—
a religion grown full of ending & empty of
time. Blue light
came up. My first were the Phoenicians it hummed
as it looked around to see if we would let it stay
here for a
while.
Its engine idled.
A beautiful day on earth.
The dirt path rattled again. Could it be tanks after all I thought.
The wind moved the trees this way and that.
We are at peace here.
The great pulsation has passed, has it not.
How could I have imagined tanks.
It must have been construction trucks.
For the more.
More I hear in the rustling
as I keep going forward. More.
*Whom
are you*

at peace with
says the tribulation drone moving among the low
clouds faster now.
The limbs awaiting Spring click & chuckle. An army of
migrating robins
lands on the field
as I go. *Whose peace*, it persists
as the sharp wind rounds the corner.
My path dips. The horizon threatens to dis-
appear, then it
disappears. Assume yr role the understories
whisper. What is it hurts you so. Do not be weak. An eagle whirls
in the updraft.
The abandoned wheelchair I always pass
is further overgrown with
vines. My shadow disappears again.
I prefer when it sticks around.
I eye the swift cumulus.
Why won't it go on, leave be,
hovering again above me now, then
under. What was
happiness it asks almost grazing the exposed
roots. Someone must be burning
wood. I remember
what it was like to make coffee in the
mornings. I remember mornings. To fall asleep
for no reason
unafraid.
The water rose a lot that last year.
Maybe it would finally take the place of pain
we thought,
filling all our still-wild underground passages.
Give me back health I think.
Give me back the wisdom of not-knowing
outcome.
Then here it is again, the trembling ground, the
sound of tanks, it cld be miles of tanks,

but no, it says, close yr eyes, let them come again, the fuel truck, the FedEx van,
the tree-trimmers arriving for the property next door—
listen, it says,
somewhere bread rises, somewhere a person is alone & checks
the time, listen, somewhere copper prices are being de-
termined, somewhere a decision is being taken—
what are they deciding I ask, trying not to hear—
the angel hovers insistently—
the trembling does not stop—
a decision is being taken re the
squatters, the tinkers, the renters, the
furloughed—some will be re-
moved, some get a
handout, we will have to see
which, some will be divided up & sold, some
will be weighed & their teeth
checked,
the power will be cut, or is it the paycheck
cut, the pages of the story
cut, or the hand
at its wrist, the tongue at its root—look
someone cuts in line—
hunger will
do that—
the trembling does not stop,
decisions are being taken,
a bid is placed,
a child is handed over now,
they turn the sound down,
you can't hear the screaming
though u can see it,
they are skipping ahead,
the drone was right there I think looking around,
and also right
here. The trembling
reminds me

of what.
To whom do I report this.
To whom do I recount this.
Then mists come in. Settle. Months go
by. Eventually, close up, a red bud
whose name is long gone,
whose genus, species, variety lifted back off it,
grows gradually less
hard &
loosens &
completely
unfurls.

WHY

you ask me
again—why
putting your tiny hand on
the not yet

unsheathed
bud on the
rhododendron,
and I see

I need to be sky
I need to be soil
there are no words
for why that I

can find fast
enough, why
you say at
the foot of the cherry's wide

blossomfall
is it dead now why
did it let go, *why,*
tossed out

into what appears
to be silence
when I say
let's run the

rain is starting—why
are we lost why did
we just leave
where we just

were why is
everything
so far behind
now as we go on I

see you think
when you reach
me again to ask
why when I say

are you coming now &

you say no,
I want to stay, I want
things to stay, I do
not want to come

away from things—what
is this we are
entering—me taking yr
hand now to speed

our going
as fast as we can in this suddenly
hard rain, yr
hand not letting go

of the rose pebble u found
feeling the first itching of
personal luck as
you now slowly

pocket it thinking
you have taken
with you a piece of
what u could not

leave behind. It is
why we went there
and left there.
It is your why.

for Samantha

THIS VASE OF QUINCE BRANCHES YOU SENT ME

in blossom. On the
kitchen table now.
Taller than me.
Why do I feel

ashamed.
In my warm vest and winter coat.
In tears.
Hands empty at my

side. What are you
for. Standing there as if in
some other country. An
otherwise. Without

past or future.
No logic religion sorrow
thought. Whispering
smoke signals to

morninglight.
Are you hearing each other. The sight of me
is of a thing with
too much heart,

too much—

salmon-pink blossoms brutal with
refusal of
meaning—why
am I

ashamed. Dear
tree,
I have watched
where u welled up and broke skin to

emerge like a disaster
of beauty, yr
tall arms here reach up &
out

differently, cut branches carefully criss-
crossed in the vase to arrange u, to hold u
firm in the
design. And the water

which you draw in at
each white
cut. I struggle
to stand at

appropriate
attention. Yr sweet acrid scent
reaches me
now. Something else

floats in the air
around yr blossoms.
It stares at me.
It keeps on staring. If it's

screaming
I can't tell. It's not domesticated.
The rest of yr tree arrives like a bloodshot eye
in my head. Silence is

stretching. There is less and less
time. I breathe
quietly. I place my hands on my
eyes. If I am a messenger, what is

my message. I fear
it is fruitless. It is un-
yielding. It is devoid of
patience. I reach

out. My fingers try for
no damage. But my mind is still here.
It envelops everything.
I think of the invisible stars. I try to

unthink them. I would give that
unthought space back
to yr branches.
Some of yr buds are

darker & swollen.
They have not opened yet.
What is it to open.
What is it to open & have one's

last time left.
The green is coming. It is pushing from behind.
I can feel the tremor of hanging on.
I have not yet fallen.

How crowded we are on our stalk.

THE QUIET

before the storm is
the storm. Our waiting tunneling outward, chewing at the as-yet-not-here, wild,
& in it the
not-yet,
that phantom, hovering, scribbling hints in the dusty airshafts where we
await rain which
once again will not come, though something we think of as *the storm*
will. Steeped in no-color color. Smothering hopes with false
promises, as wind comes up and we feel our soul turn frantic
in us, craning this way and that, yes the soul can twist, can winch itself into knots,
why not, there is light but no warmth, we are alone yet
not, no trace but the feeling of
trace, who wouldn't be a child again,
teach me how to work, how to be kind, teach me ignorance, sweet ignorance,
the roads lie down in us, all the roads taken, they knot up,
they went nowhere, cld that be true,
they made a shapeless burden we carried around calling it lived-
experience. Did you live. Did it feel like life to
you. At the water's edge you feel
you should ask for
instruction. Go ahead. Right there where the waves shatter over the rocks and the plumes
rise, the vast silky roads of ocean arrive as spray, spume, droplets, foam.
Is that shattering what was meant by ripeness.
We were told to aim for ripeness,
to be broken into
wisdom. You look at the rocks again, the sleeping planet at your back, under yr
feet, nothing coming back, nothing coming round, you close yr eyes
for clues, u peer, inhale, listen madly for clues. What is hell. The
imagination of what is
coming is hell. The light of my monitor
blinks. What will the readout
tell us. Who is us. How will *us* change
when the readout

arrives, the ice-core update, the new temps for the
arctic depth-sounds, bone scans, outposts on
stars, on cells. I look for the stars on
my body, I look all over. The spray off the rock
rinses my face. My
eyes take the brine. What
is coming, will you be there. In this quiet now is
all of
yr life says the monitor, should I say *my*
life, should I say
ours, I can't tell tenses & pronouns
apart, I can feel
my veins, I shake in my dreams, I think I am cold, the wind picks up,
like a tooth on a stone, the tooth of something small
which was slaughtered,
its screaming
below the threshold of our
hearing, just below. Then maybe I'm not born yet. Maybe I am waiting in
the canal. Can you
hear me I say again. They are putting a drug in.
They want me to join the
human
race. They know we are out of time.
Hurry they say. A different kind of hurry than the one you
are used to
they say.
They are trying to tame us.
Outside I hear laughter but it could be veins rushing when
guns are pointed. They are pointed at the outside of
this. At the belly of
this poem. They can't help
it. They are in cities under
siege. Their hands on the triggers are
hopeless. They have run out of
ideas. Dogs run through the streets till they
turn to meat.
The things that live in the ground

have to surface.
The heat outside sounds like air sucking up
light. They are calling my name. I am not born yet & still I am trying
to say yes, yes,
here I am,
is there a bloodied envelope for me,
one of us needs to be delivered. Now a beam is shining over all the rubble
picking for clues.
Is this all the life left before the gate to
the next-on thing?
They tell me the gate to the next-on thing is bloody but warm.
That they mean well.
To remember that they
meant well.
A seedpod floats down, swirling light on & off.
The shadows want to show us
wind. *Even the invisible*
say the shadows
is here. Are you
here?
Was that a butterfly or its shadow just now. The lake
dried up. The earth is
on standby. No, the earth is going off
standby. The mode is shifting. A switch is
being thrown. The passengers
are stranded. Will there be enough. Of
anything. Look,
the girl is sitting on her small suitcase
weeping. She is alone now.
Look, she is no longer weeping. She is
staring. The earth says
it is time. Everyone checks their watch.
Your destination is in sight. Be
ready. Brace. The traincars shake. They rattle.
Our test is still blinking.
Is this the ending rattling. The outcome. The verified

result. No
it is something else that rattles.
How I wish there were an intermission.
The sweets would arrive on their little wooden trays.
The curtain's velvet would descend.
To let the story cool off
for a while.
So we could catch up,
compare our favorite parts,
wonder who would be saved,
who would pay the price in full,
for their folly, their trespass, their refusal, their
love. No, I remember learning,
back in the prior era,
there is no love. It's all
desire. Hurry up. Your destination's
in sight. Brace for
arrival. The traincars
shake. They rattle.
No it's something else that rattles.
I shake you gently. This would be a good time to
rouse. Do you wish
to rouse.
Are we there yet you ask. I do not know. I am
the poem. I am just shaking you
gently to remind you.
Of what? Of time? That this is time? That there is
time. Do you want
the results. No. I don't want to know.
The lake went by so quickly.
It was teeming, as they used to say, then it was
sand. Then even the sand blew away.
And now look. It is
bone. How it shines.
The people in the committee meeting don't see the lake, they are
still talking. Actually

they are not talking.
They are
screaming.
They do this by looking
down. The lakebed goes by in a flash
on their overhead.
Whose turn is it now.
Have you stood your turn in line.
Have you voted.
For what says the young eagle
diving over the lake looking for the lake
as the train rattles by, for what.

DAWN 2040

These tiny sounds
you think you hear
in the house
elsewhere—

is someone awake, is
someone alive. You
turn around. *Just
now*, you hear

yourself say. I know
what finished is.
I know the *just
now* & then the *just*

gone. I am alive.
Then it is the sun
arriving, rising
just above the edge

of yr turning, my
earth. It's touching my
shoulder. *You*
it makes me feel,

you. Are you there.
In this world now, this
is the last
moment in which

we can breathe
normally. *Normally* I say
to myself.
The scrub oaks

are dying
back. The white sky
arrives, whitening
further. Did we

survive at the end
of this story, I ask
the sun. I give up on
tenses here. What were

the things we called
freedoms, I
ask. But the sun
as it rises is touching

everything less and less
tenderly, reaching
everything,
no matter how u

hide, no water
anywhere—though here, listen,
I make it
for you—*drip drip*—

as I admire yr breathing
wherever u are now
reading this. Inhale.
Are you still there

the sun says to me
as I hide on this
page. Be there,
as long as you can,

take it, be there
as I rise. The lifting
groundmist now
the last moment,

the very last, in which

you can breathe. Soon—
now actually—
you must hide
from me. You. You

beautiful thing, you
human, yr lungs
I can crush with one
inadvertent in-

halation. But how
I admired yr
breathing, yr so few
years, how u took them

to heart and believed in
things to the
end. The end is
a hard thing to

comprehend. You
did not
comprehend it. Now go,
I must widen

across the fields,

the cicadas will soon
begin in unison
the song of unison
till u can hear no more

variation, no rise or
fall. Can I live please
in this unchanging sound, I
ask, as we enter further

into yr dayrise.
What was that
just flew over. What else is
in here. I sit as quietly

as breathing
permits. All's
hum & insect
thread. Nothing un-

locks. Yes there's burning
wind sometimes, but all
is building towards
sand's hard thought, nothing will

change its mind
this dune of the future
as it moves
towards us

here where we can for now
still hide. You there,
wondering what to do with
yr day,

yawning as you wake
from dream,
I can almost make you out
in yr brightening

morning-light. You there. Wake up. But
nobody's here,
just the earth
revolving, in-

exhaustible, without

purpose, in which
from moment to
moment
even now

change gathers,
inception gathers, & variation, & pro-
liferation—
And all is. All is.

Do you remember.

CODA

THEN THE RAIN

after years of virga, after
much *almost*
& much *never again*, after
coalescing in dry

lightning & downdrafts & fire,
after taking an alternate
path thru
history & bypassing

us, after the trees,
after the gardens,
after the hard seeds
pushed in as deep as

possible & kept alive on dew,
after the ruts
which it had once cut
filled in with

dust & molds—& pods
that cannot sprout—
not even the birds
came—& old roads

began to reappear—

after the animals,
after the smallest creatures
in their tunnels & under
their rocks,

after it all went, then,
one day,
out of in-
terference & dis-

continuity, out of in-
congruity,
out of collision
somewhere high above our

burnt lands, out of
chemistry, unknowable
no matter how
quantifiable,

out of the touching of one atom by an
other, out of the
accident of
touch, the rain

came.

We thought it was
more wind. Something tapped
the peeling roof.
We knew it was not

heat ticking, our secret imaginary
birds. We knew it by the smell which filled
the air re-
minding us, what did it

remind us of, that smell,

as if the air turned green,
as if the air were the deep in-
side of the earth
we can never reach

where *it* reaches out to
those constellations we have not
discovered, not named, & now
never will,

and which are not dead, no—

And it brought memory. But of
what. So long. Where are you my
tenses. The crowns
rattled again, harder, & again we thought

wind. I pressed
the rusted screen-door
& stepped out. Was I afraid? Where it hit
dust whirled up

in miles of refusals—stringy, flaring,
as if flames could be dust,
faster with each landing, till it
tamed them & they

lay down again as earth,
and were still,
and took it in
everywhere,

& when I sat on the low wall
it slid over my features,
& my neck held runnels,
as if I were a small book

being carefully perused for
faults, ridges, lapses of
time in my thought—
because I could not recall it—

my skin could not,

my hands could not,

I look at them now

with my eyes full of rain,
and they say hold us up,
you are not dying
yet, we are

alive in the death
of this iteration of
earth, there will be another
in which no creatures like us

walk on this
plateau of years & minutes & grasses &
roads, a place where
no memory can form, no memory of

anything, not again, but for now
the windowpanes shake as the
harder rain hits
and the stiff grasses bend over &

the thing which had been a meadow once
releases a steam,
& if you listen you can hear
a faint pulse in it,

a mirage, a release of seeds into the air

where wind insists, & my heavy

hands which rise now, palms up, shining,
say to me,
touch, touch it all,
start with your face,

put your face in us.

ACKNOWLEDGMENTS

Grateful acknowledgment to the editors of the following journals and magazines in which these poems first appeared: *The London Review of Books, The New York Review of Books, The New Yorker, The Yale Review, The New Republic.*

More than ever this book would not be possible without the friendship and guidance of many people, in particular Ty Romijn, Sandra Washburne, Lucia Hayman, Kevin Cain, Edward Youkilis, Tara Ledden, Will Ledden, John Ledden, Elisa Veschini, Dale Lanzone, James Dougherty, Steve Bickley, Leroy Harrison, Lila DiBiasio, Josh Scott, Jim Parr, James Barron, Jeannette Montgomery Barron, Paola Peroni, Amy Hempel, Marcela del Carmen, Ursula Matulonis, Alessandra Lorusso, Tom Neilan, Chris Gilligan, Kenneth Gold, Mary Alice Robinson, and Jeffrey Zack.

To Tim Phillips, Jane Miller, Cal Bedient, Helen Vendler, Kamran Javadizadeh, Daniel Soar, Jana Prikryl, Kevin Young, Hannah Aizenman, Antonella Francini, Terry Tempest Williams, Geralyn Dreyfous, Josh Bell, Tracy K. Smith, Michael Pollan, Judith Belzer, Teju Cole, Forrest Gander, D.A. Powell, Geraldine Brooks, Saskia Hamilton, Emily Braun, and Carol Gilligan, thank you for being there.

To Sol Kim Bentley—thank you for your brilliant advice, and your eagle eye: every word here has been read, edited, copyedited, and proofed by you. To Erica Mena, thank you for your design genius, and for never saying no, no matter how late and interminable the revision; and thank you for your encouragement and example. To Case Kerns and Lauren Bimmler, bless you for your friendship.

To Michael Wiegers, Ryo Yamaguchi, Claretta Holsey, and the whole crew at Copper Canyon Press, thank you, as we start down this new path together, for your profoundly intelligent devotion to the art.

To Stephen, Emily, Alvaro, Samantha, and Peter, I could not have made this without you.

ABOUT THE AUTHOR

Jorie Graham is the author of fifteen collections of poems. Her poetry has been widely translated and has been the recipient of numerous awards, among them the Pulitzer Prize, the Forward Prize (UK), the Los Angeles Times Book Award, the International Nonino Prize, and the Rebekah Johnson Bobbitt National Prize for Poetry from the Library of Congress. She lives in Massachusetts and teaches at Harvard University.

More information is available at www.joriegraham.com.

Poetry is vital to language and living. Since 1972, Copper Canyon Press has published extraordinary poetry from around the world to engage the imaginations and intellects of readers, writers, booksellers, librarians, teachers, students, and donors.

WE ARE GRATEFUL FOR THE MAJOR SUPPORT PROVIDED BY:

academy of american poets

THE PAUL G. ALLEN
FAMILY FOUNDATION

amazon literary partnership

4 CULTURE

the point
envision · enact · evolve

Lannan

ART WORKS.
National Endowment for the Arts
arts.gov

WASHINGTON STATE
ARTS COMMISSION

A&
OFFICE OF ARTS & CULTURE
SEATTLE

The Witter Bynner Foundation
for Poetry

TO LEARN MORE ABOUT UNDERWRITING
COPPER CANYON PRESS TITLES,
PLEASE CALL 360-385-4925 EXT. 103

WE ARE GRATEFUL FOR THE MAJOR SUPPORT PROVIDED BY:

Richard Andrews and Colleen
    Chartier
Anonymous
Jill Baker and Jeffrey Bishop
Anne and Geoffrey Barker
Donna Bellew
Matthew Bellew
Sarah Bird
Will Blythe
John Branch
Diana Broze
Sarah Cavanaugh
Keith Cowan and Linda Walsh
Stephanie Ellis-Smith and
    Douglas Smith
Mimi Gardner Gates
Gull Industries Inc. on behalf of
    William True
The Trust of Warren A. Gummow
William R. Hearst III
Carolyn and Robert Hedin
David and Jane Hibbard
Bruce S. Kahn
Phil Kovacevich and Eric Wechsler
Lakeside Industries Inc. on behalf
    of Jeanne Marie Lee

Maureen Lee and Mark Busto
Peter Lewis and Johanna Turiano
Ellie Mathews and Carl Youngmann
    as The North Press
Larry Mawby and Lois Bahle
Hank and Liesel Meijer
Jack Nicholson
Petunia Charitable Fund and
    adviser Elizabeth Hebert
Madelyn Pitts
Suzanne Rapp and Mark Hamilton
Adam and Lynn Rauch
Emily and Dan Raymond
Joseph C. Roberts
Jill and Bill Ruckelshaus
Cynthia Sears
Kim and Jeff Seely
Nora Hutton Shepard
D.D. Wigley
Joan F. Woods
Barbara and Charles Wright
In honor of C.D. Wright,
    from Forrest Gander
Caleb Young as C. Young Creative
The dedicated interns and faithful
    volunteers of Copper Canyon Press

The pressmark for Copper Canyon Press
suggests entrance, connection, and interaction
while holding at its center
an attentive, dynamic space for poetry.

This book is set in Arno.
Cover design by Gopa & Ted2, Inc.
Book design by Erica Mena.
Printed on archival-quality paper.